Alexander Peskanov's
THE RUSSIAN TECHNICAL REGIMEN
FOR THE PIANO

(Series of Six Books)

SCALES IN SINGLE NOTES

Technical Editor - Lynn Radcliffe

© MCMXCI By The Willis Music Company
International Copyright Secured
Printed in U.S.A

To
My Beloved Teachers in Russia,
ROSALIA MOLODIETZKAYA and her son, EMIL

IN GRATEFUL REMEMBRANCE

Concert pianist and composer, appeared as soloist with London Philharmonic, English Chamber Orchestra, National Symphony and orchestras of Baltimore, St. Louis, Houston, Utah and others. Concertized in 48 states and 20 countries on four continents. Recipient of ASCAP awards for music and theater compositions. Graduated from Stoliarsky School of Music, Odessa, Ukraine, and received Masters Degree from Julliard School of Music, New York. Married to Lu Ann, concert flutist and teacher; has five children.

ALEXANDER PESKANOV

Author

Music/piano enthusiast, retired from career in the aerospace industry. Was record reviewer for American Record Guide Magazine, artist. Graduated with BS degree from Syracuse University, 1942. Married to Jean; has two children.

LYNN E. RADCLIFFE

Technical Editor

* * * * * * * * * * * * * * * * * * * *

Lynn Radcliffe and I started our relationship with a fair exchange: he told me about traveling in space and I told him about playing double thirds and broken chords. Lynn was one of the first people to whom I introduced elements of the Russian Technical Regimen for piano. Each of us added a new dimension to the other's life, and we found that we shared one significant quality in our characters: endless curiosity in the pursuit of knowledge. Discovering that this regimen is just as effective for a person of sixty-eight and beyond as it is for a child of ten has inspired us to write this series of books for students of all ages.

Alexander Peskanov

FOREWORD

This exercise volume is part of a series of books entitled *The Russian Technical Regimen for the Piano*. It consists of the INTRODUCTION AND GUIDE to the regimen and five exercise volumes. The Russian Technical Regimen encompasses all the technical requirements which have been in use in Russian and Soviet music schools and conservatories for more than a century.

This exercise presents twenty-four single-note scales in the Russian pattern with transitions, and chromatic scales - also in the Russian pattern. The major scales appear in the circle of fifths with the relative harmonic minor scales in between. This is an excellent exercise that developes great stamina, concentration and coordination between mind, wrist and fingers. To fully understand how to learn and practice this "twenty-four scale" exercise, one should study Chapter IV of THE INTRODUCTION AND GUIDE to *The Russian Technical Regimen for the Piano*.

The single-note chromatic scales are presented in four configurations: (1) octaves, (2) thirds, (3) tenths, and (4) sixths. Chapter V of the INTRODUCTION AND GUIDE illustrates the various stages of development in playing these scales.

In all phases of *The Russian Technical Regimen for the Piano* accents must always be the foundation for the rhythm and points of relaxation. The benefits of the Regimen can accrue only if it is practiced in the proper manner with full realization of the Guide Book instructions.

Alexander Peskanov

Supplementary materials and additional teaching aids include:

Broken Chords

Russian Broken Chords

Arpeggios and Broken Chords

Scales in Double Notes: Thirds, Sixths, Octaves

Instructional Videos, "In Search of Sound"
        Produced by Classical Video Concepts, Inc.

Piano Olympics Kit, Manual and Demonstration Video
        Produced by CVC, Inc.

TWENTY–FOUR SINGLE-NOTE SCALES IN RUSSIAN PATTERN WITH TRANSITIONS

F MAJOR

Transition to D minor
(21 to go)

G MINOR
(harmonic)

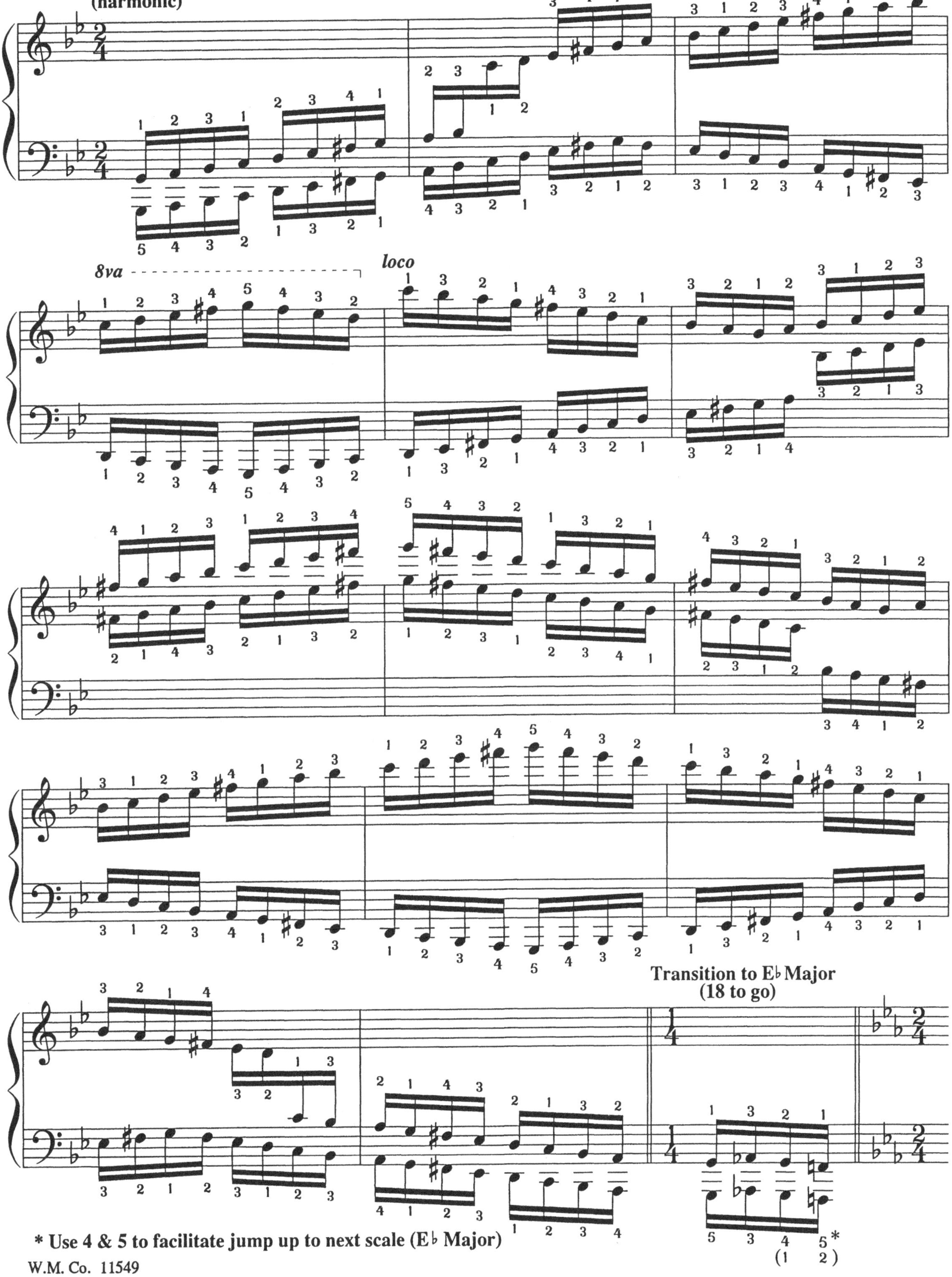
8va
loco
Transition to E♭ Major
(18 to go)

*** Use 4 & 5 to facilitate jump up to next scale (E♭ Major)**

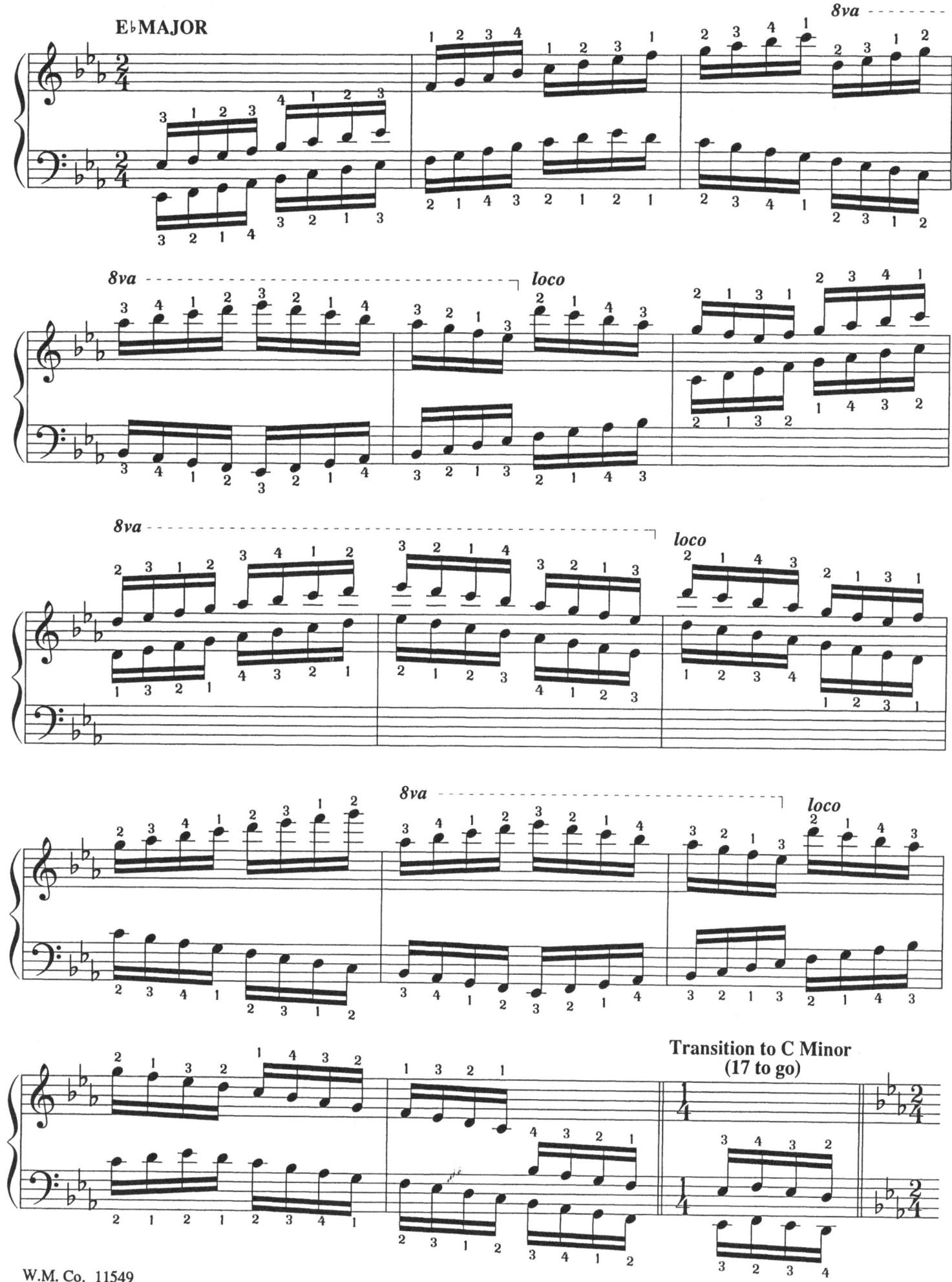

F MINOR (harmonic)

Transition to D♭ Major (14 to go)

*Use 2 & 1 (R.H.) and 4 & 5 (L.H.) to facilitate jump up to next scale (D♭ Major).
W.M. Co. 11549

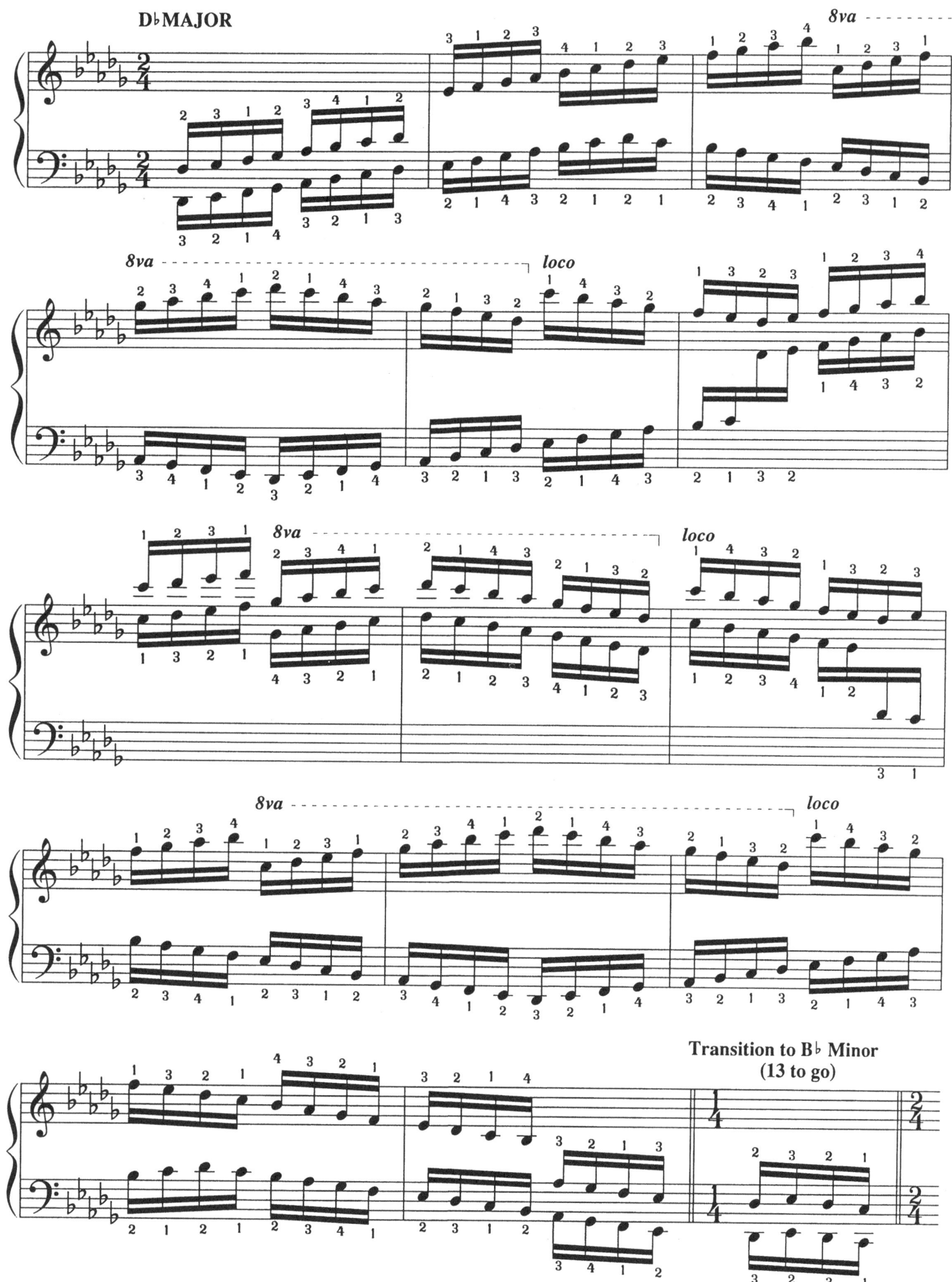

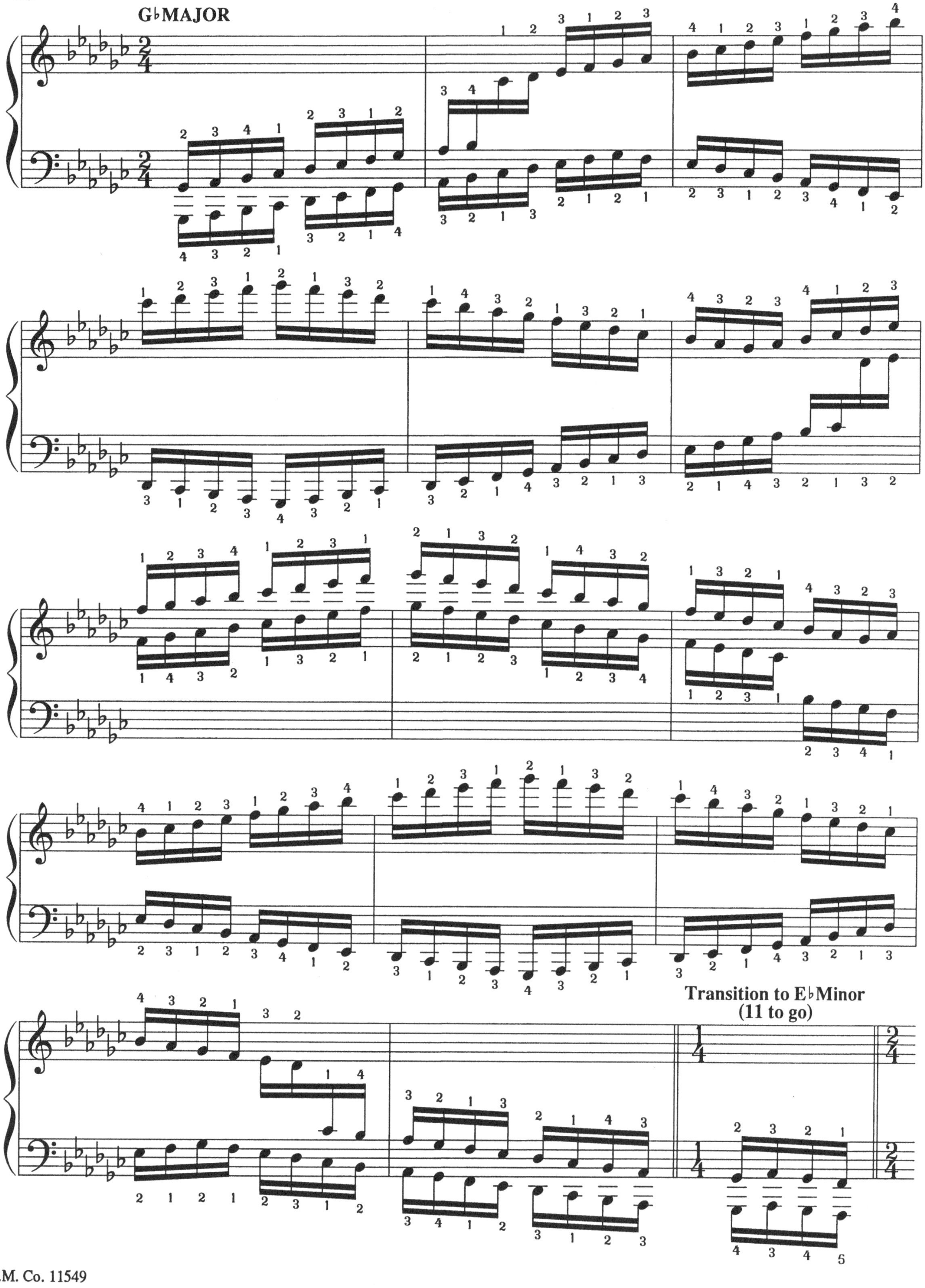
G♭MAJOR
Transition to E♭Minor
(11 to go)

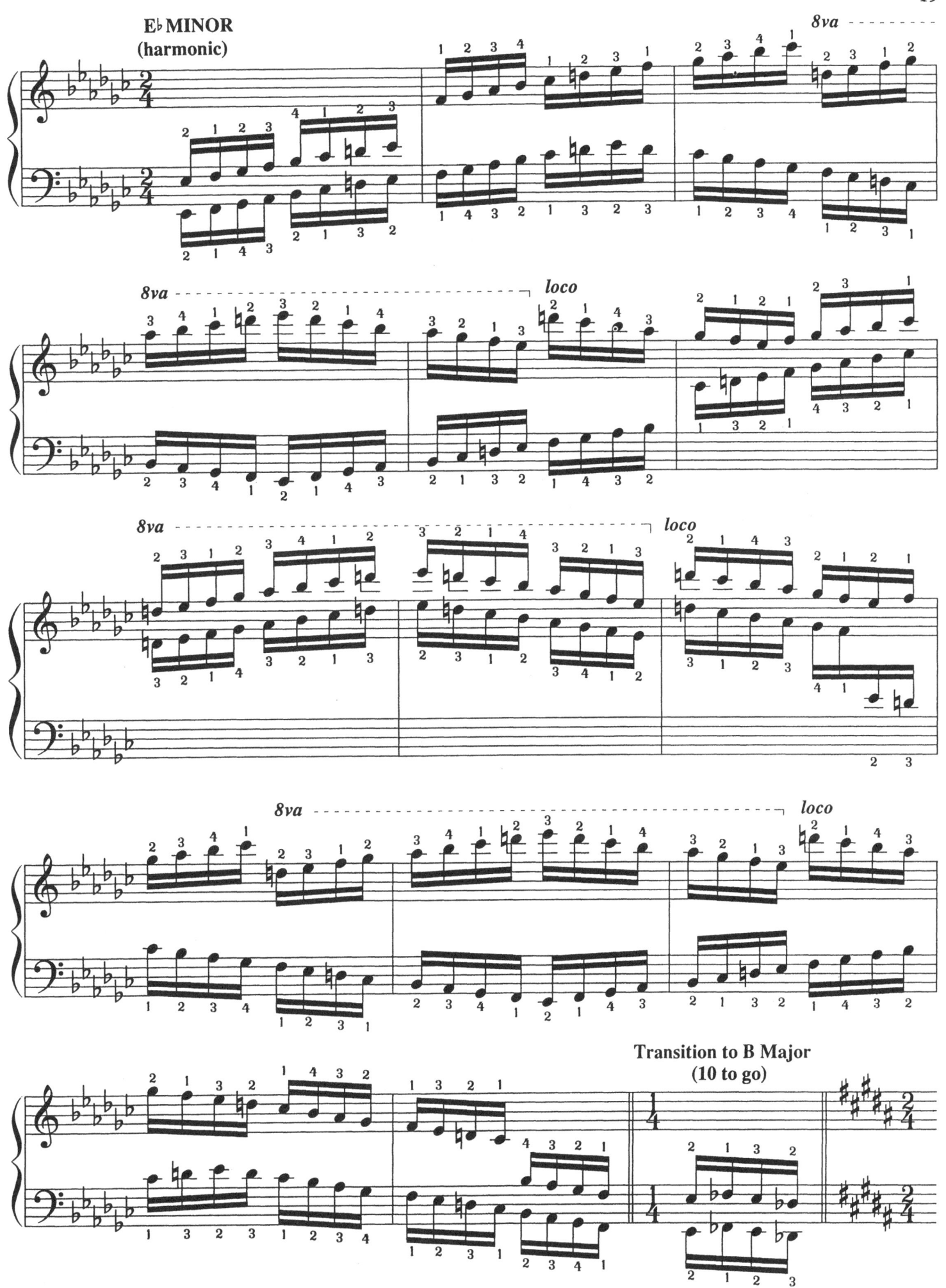

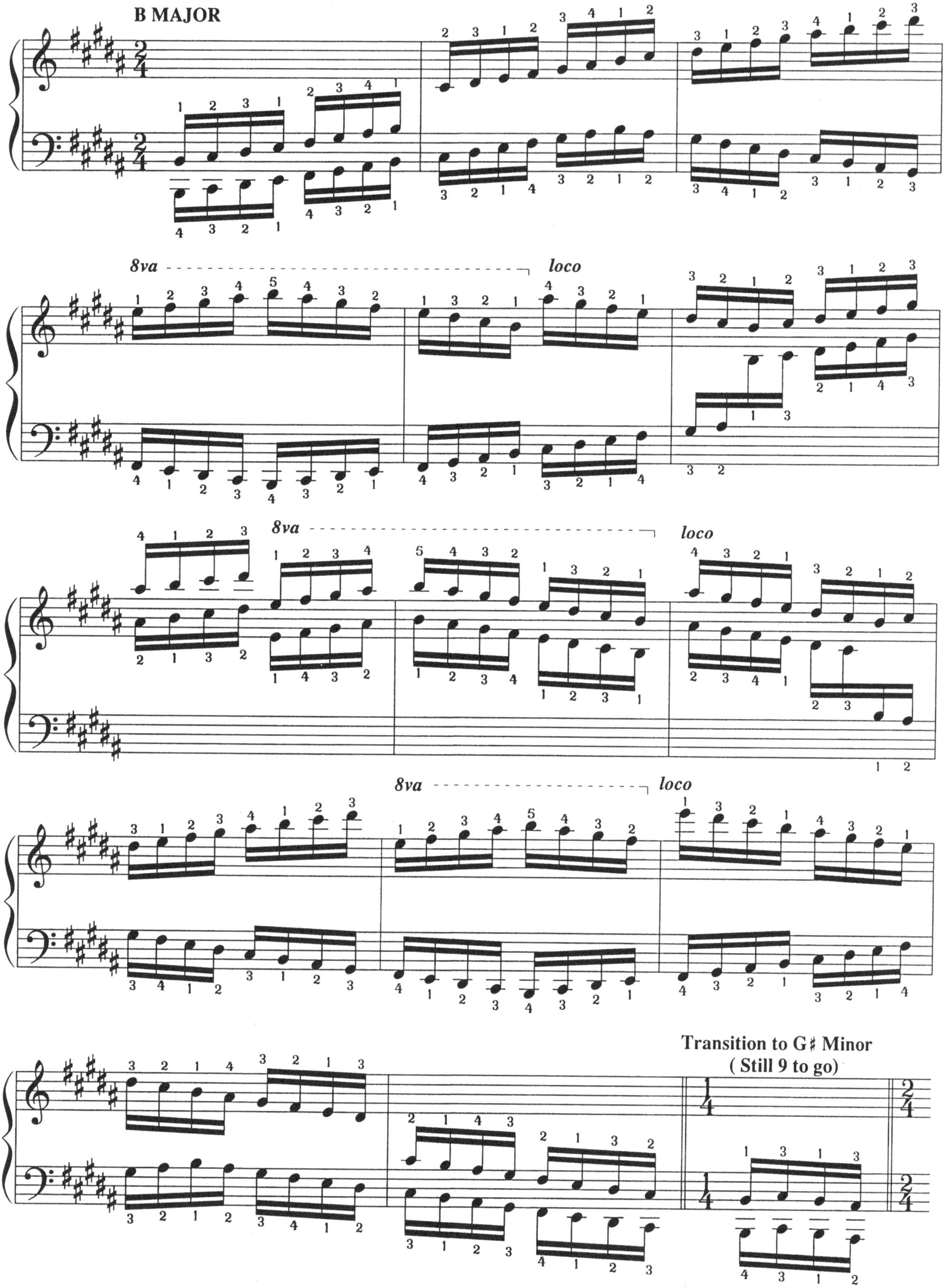

G♯ MINOR
(Harmonic)

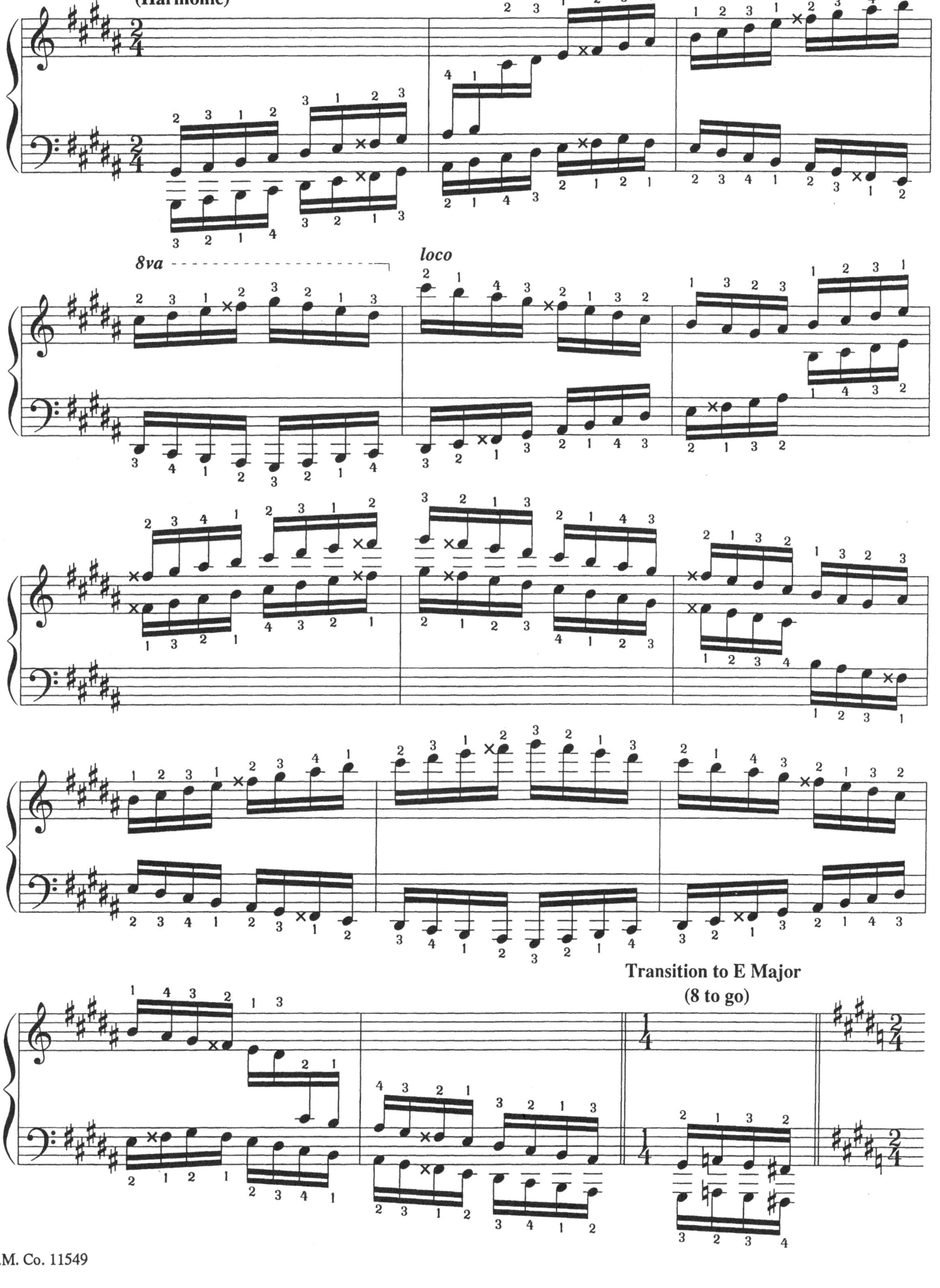
8va
loco
Transition to E Major
(8 to go)

Transition to C♯ Minor (7 to go)

* Use 2 & 1 (R.H.) and 4 & 5 (L.H.) to facilitate jump up to next scale (C♯ Minor)

E MINOR
(Harmonic)

Transition to C Major
Congratulations!
(none to go)

Want to try again?

This page is
deliberately left blank
in order to accommodate
page turns.

VARYING DYNAMICS BETWEEN THE HANDS
A MINOR - EXAMPLE SCALE
(harmonic)

Transition to F Major

SINGLE - NOTE CHROMATIC SCALES
OCTAVES

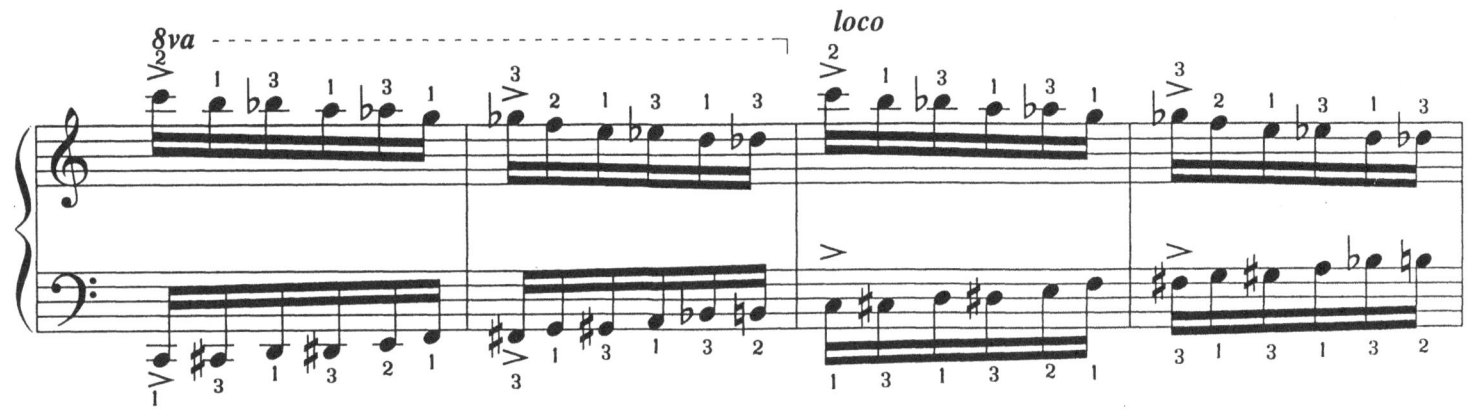

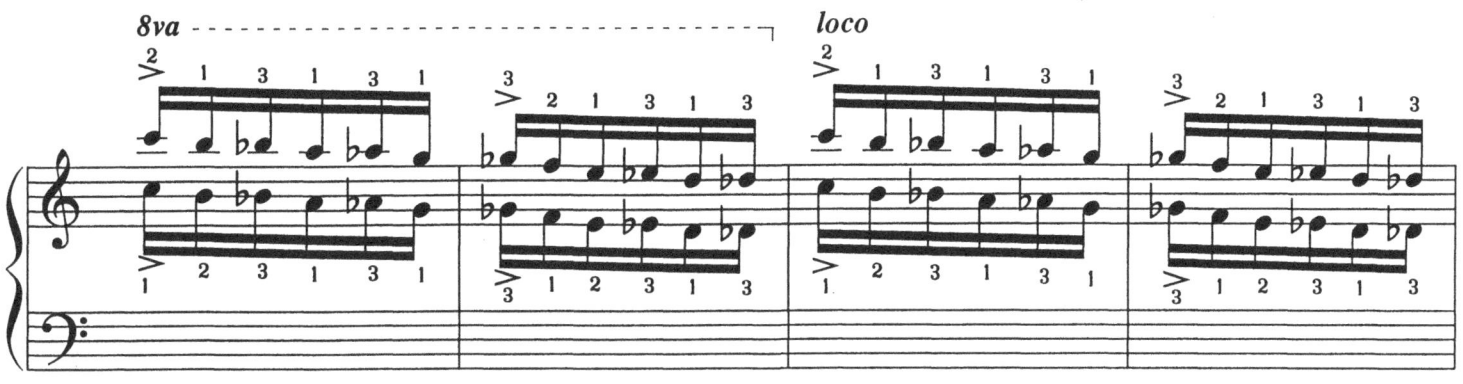

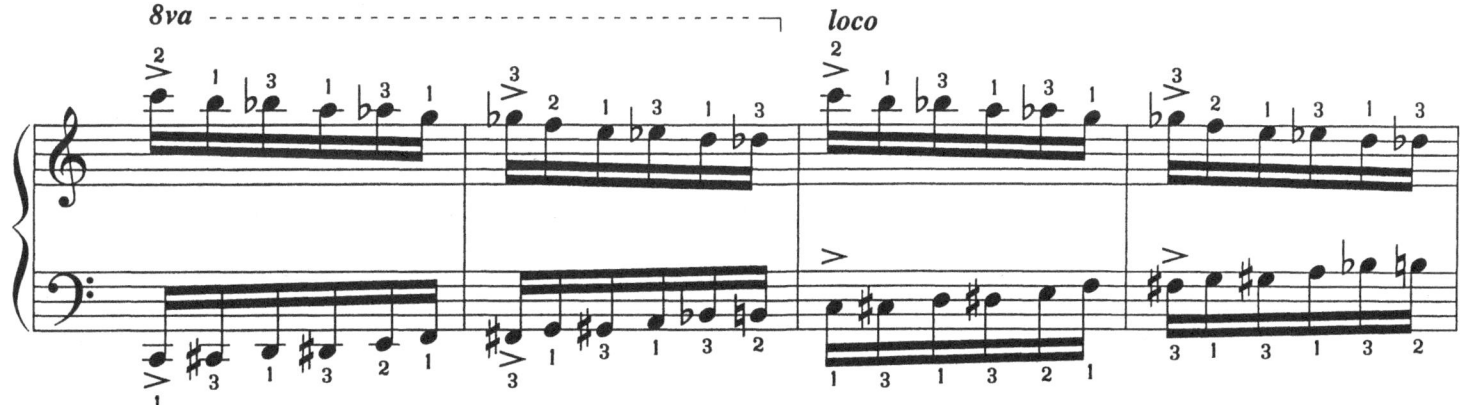
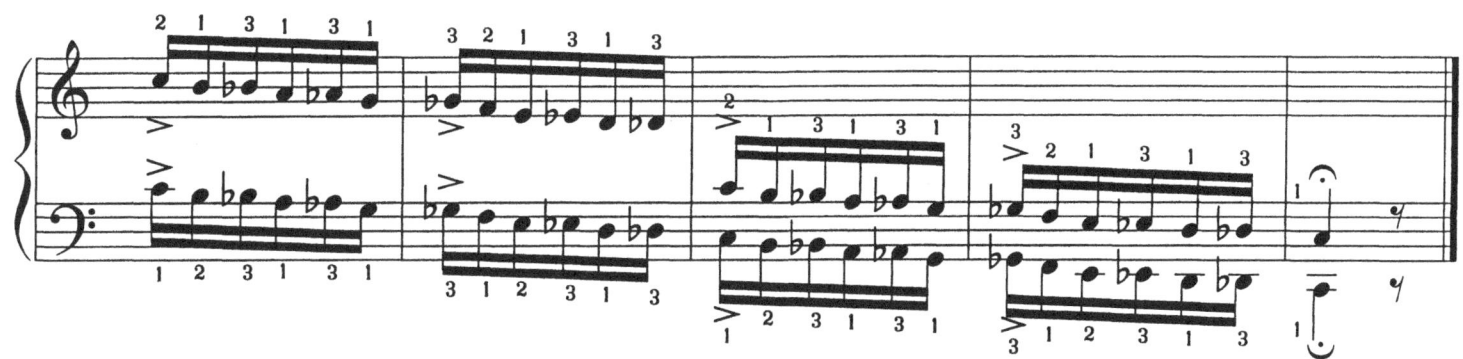

SINGLE-NOTE CHROMATIC SCALE
THIRDS

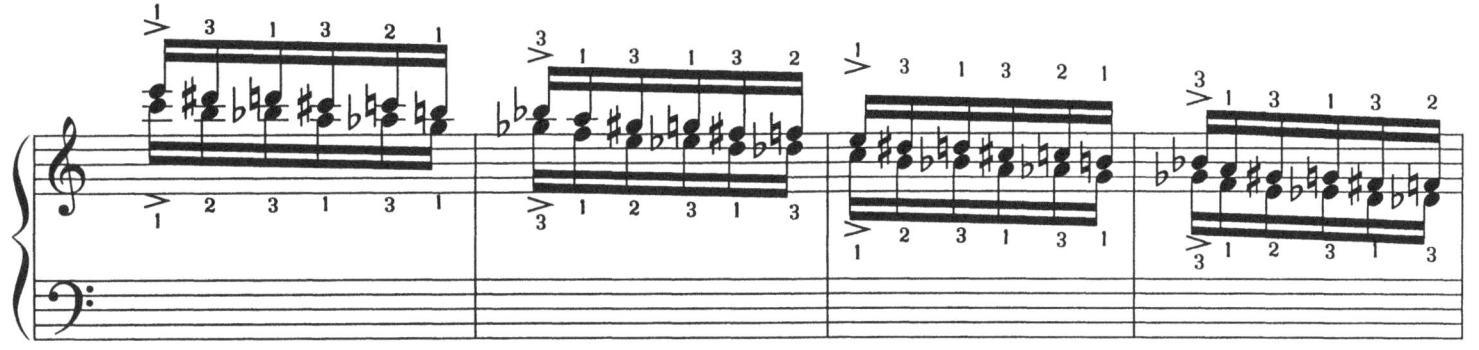
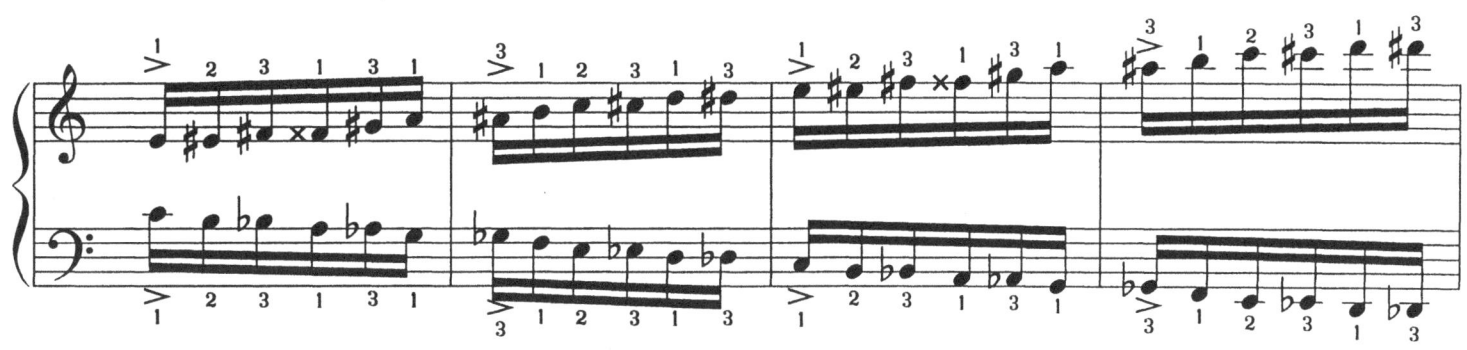
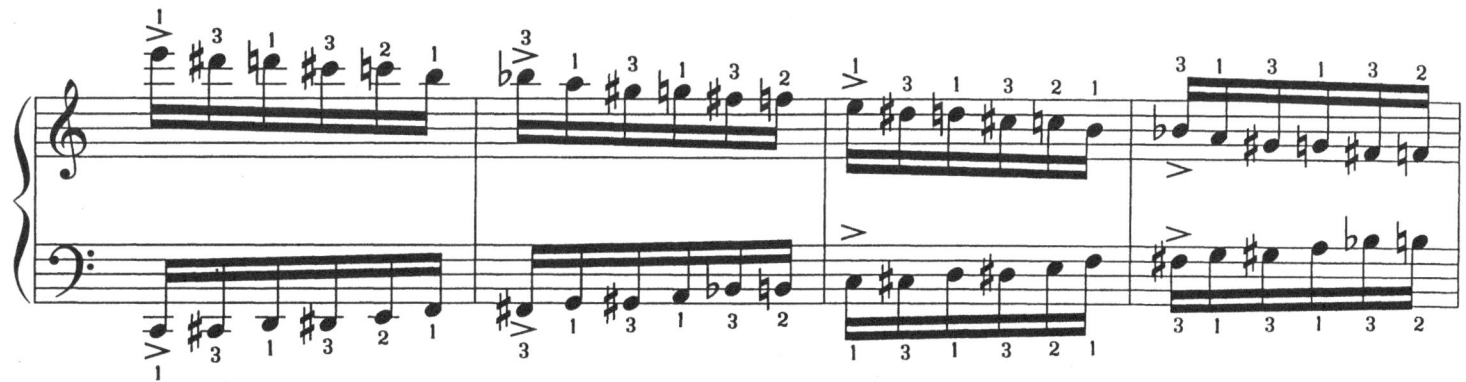
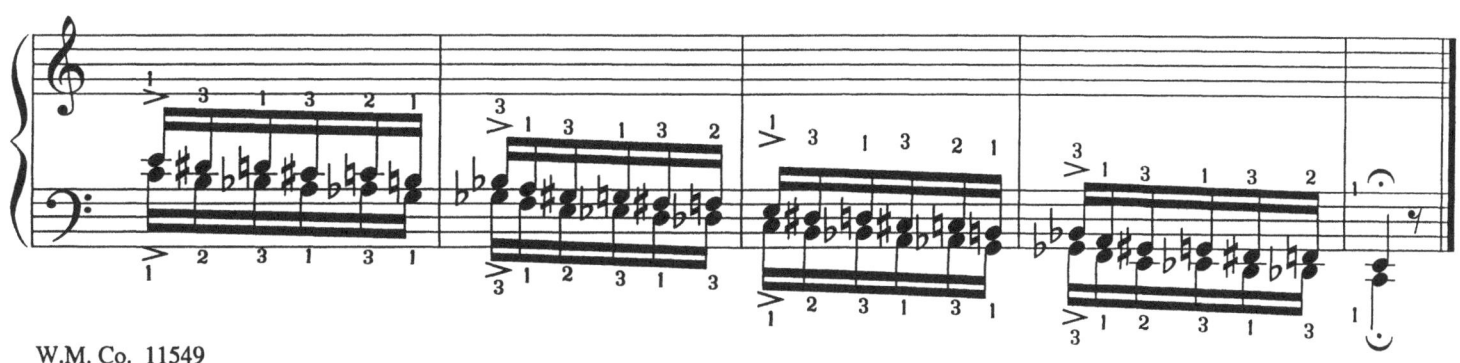

SINGLE-NOTE CHROMATIC SCALE
TENTHS

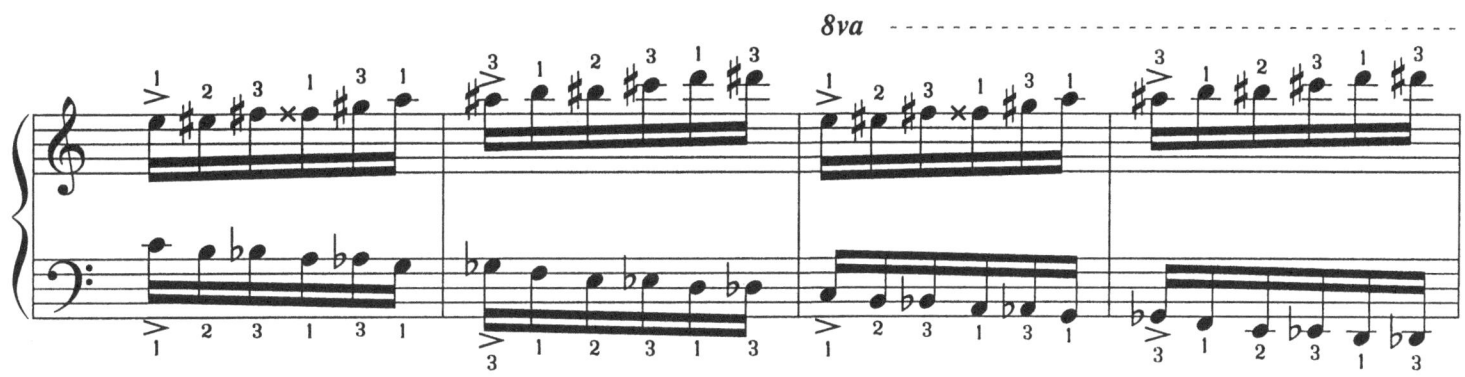
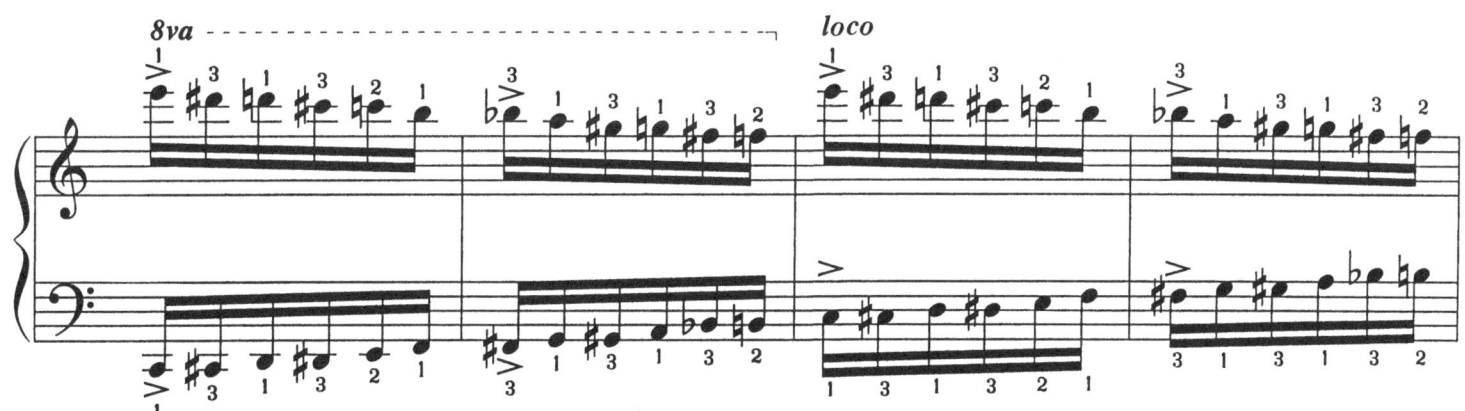
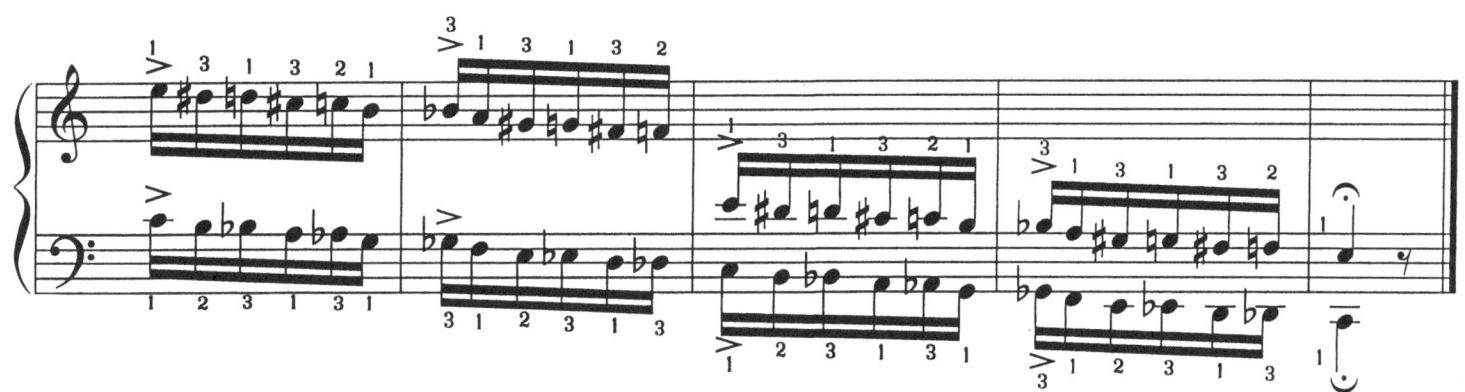

SINGLE-NOTE CHROMATIC SCALE
SIXTHS

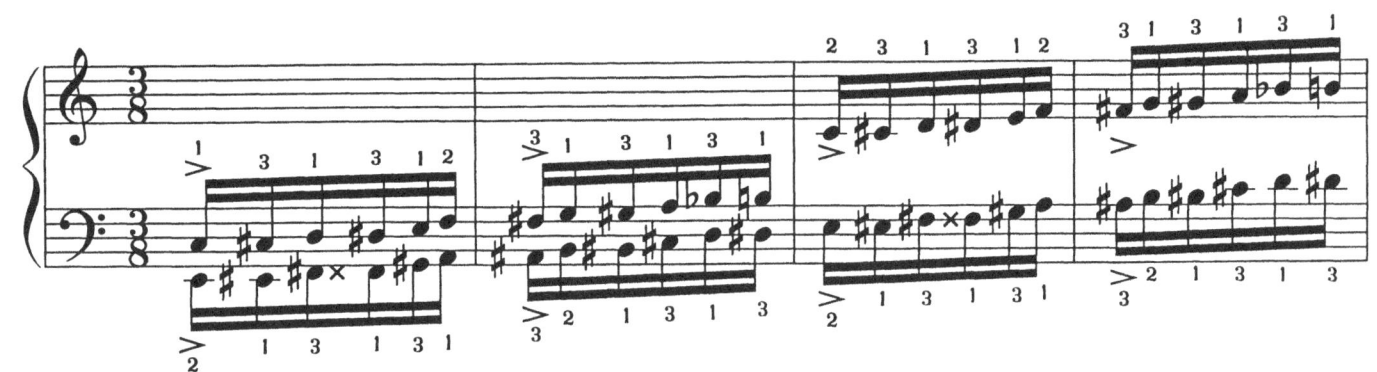

39

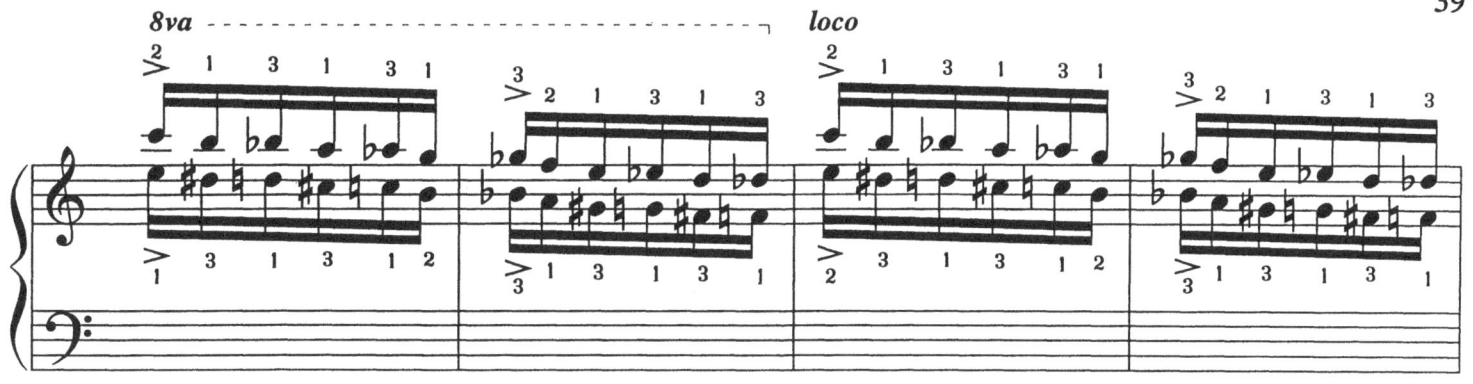

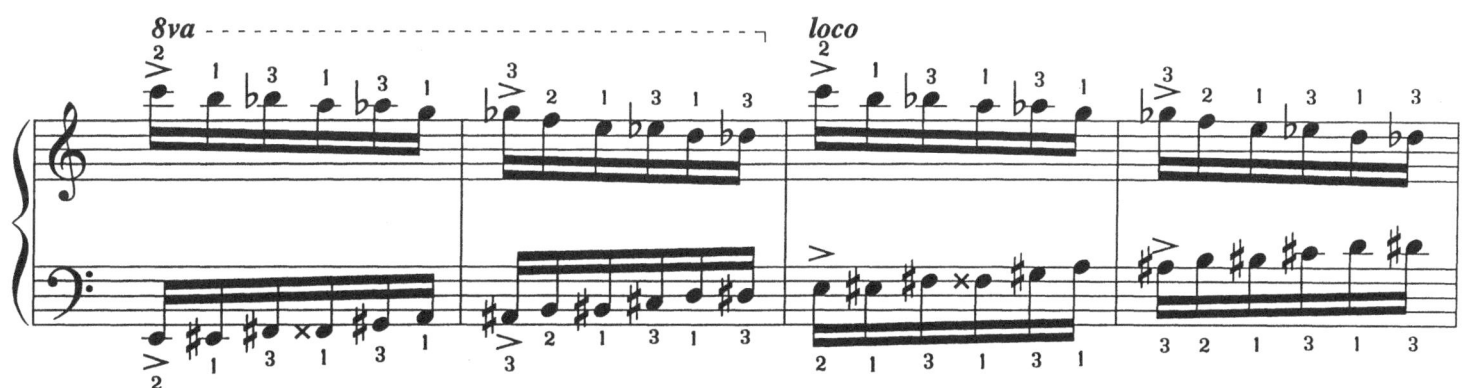

W.M. Co. 11549

Alexander Peskanov
On The Russian Technical Regimen

---Introduction & Guide ("Guide Book")

Complete instructions on how to practice the technical requirements of The Russian Technical Regimen

---Exercise Volume I, Scales in Single Notes

---Exercise Volume II, Broken Chords

---Exercise Volume III, Russian Broken Chords

---Exercise Volume IV, Arpeggios and Block Chords

---Exercise Volume V, Scales in Doubles Notes: thirds, sixths, and octaves

Instructional Videos, "In Search of Sound"
    Demonstrations and performances by Alexander Peskanov

    (produced by Classical Video Concepts, Inc.)

---Piano Olympics Kit (Manual and Video)

An exciting Piano Event that helps teachers to engage students in practicing scales and exercises using the Russian Technical Regimen. Also, it offers the opportunity to demonstrate their accomplishments in the performance of their repertoire (Produced by Classical Video Concepts, Inc.)